REGULATE ANXIETY WC KIDS

50 CBT Exercises and A Help Kids Regulate Their Emotions, Fo n the Positives, and Enhance Coping Skills for Ages 5-10

By

Sharon Lynn

Grand Publication

Legal Notice

Disclaimer Notice

This book is written and published independently. Please keep in mind that the material in this publication is solely for educational and entertaining purposes. All efforts have provided authentic, up-to-date, trustworthy, and comprehensive information. There are no express or implied assurances. The purpose of this book's material is to assist readers in having a better understanding of the subject matter. The activities, information, and exercises are provided solely for self-help information. This book is not intended to replace expert psychologists, legal, financial, or other guidance. If you require counseling, please get in touch with a qualified professional.

By reading this text, the reader accepts that the author will not be held liable for any damages, indirectly or directly, experienced due to the use of the information included herein, particularly, but not limited to, omissions, errors, or inaccuracies. As a reader, you are accountable for your decisions, actions, and consequences.

About the Author

Sharon Lynn is a certified family therapist with 7+ years of clinical experience where he has counseled a large number of families.

Having 7+ years of clinical practice in the field, he has worked on a number of issues faced by families in their day-to-day lives, such as child and adolescent behavioral problems, domestic abuse, an unexpected illness, unemployment, infidelity issues, and grieving death and separation or divorce. Helping the readers in learning about anxiety, stress, family issues, abusive behavior and emotions management are some of his topics of writings.

He focuses on the attributes of a family to differentiate between a functional and a dysfunctional one. He advises on the use of different techniques to improve family bonding.

Contents

Introduction

It is common for children to show feelings of insecurity, worry, and dread from time to time. Anxiety in children usually comes in waves and does not last long.

Different fears arise at different times in one's life. Babies and toddlers, for example, are commonly afraid of loud noises, distances, outsiders, and separation. Preschoolers may develop a fear of being alone and in the dark. School-aged youngsters may be terrified of ghosts, supernatural beings, social settings, failure, criticism, testing, and actual injury or threat.

Babies and young children are not likely to be concerned about anything. To feel concerned, youngsters must imagine the future and the negative events that may occur. This is why youngsters above the age of eight are more likely to feel worried.

As children get older, they become concerned about a variety of issues. They may be concerned about getting sick or wounded while they are young. The concentration gets less definite as children grow older and into adolescence. For example, people may spend a lot of time thinking about war, natural, economic, and political concerns, and family connections.

Anxiety disorders induce excessive fear and worry in children and changes in their behavior, sleep, food, and mood. Anxiety disorders can impact children and teenagers in various ways. They are as follows:

- Selective Mutism
- Specific Phobias
- Social Anxiety Disorder

- Panic Disorder
- Separation Anxiety Disorder
- Generalized Anxiety Disorder

A parent may notice indicators of anxiety in a kid or teen. A child might, for example, grip, skip school, or weep. They may appear afraid or upset or refuse to speak or do things. Anxiety affects children and teenagers in ways that others cannot perceive. They may get fearful, concerned, or tense due to it.

It can also have an impact on their physical well-being. They may feel anxious, shaky, or breathless. They may have stomach butterflies, a hot cheek, clammy palms, a parched tongue, or a rapid heartbeat.

The "fight or flight" reaction is responsible for these anxiety symptoms. This is the body's natural reaction to a threat.It causes the body's natural substances to be released. These chemicals are preparing us to face a serious threat. Heart rate, respiration, muscles, nerves, and digestion are all affected. This reaction is designed to keep us safe from harm. The "fight or flight" reaction is hyperactive in anxiety disorders. Even when there is no real threat, it happens.

The most common treatment for anxiety disorders is Cognitive-Behavioral Therapy (CBT). This is a sort of talk therapy that teaches families, children, and teenagers how to cope with anxiety, fear, and worry.

CBT teaches children that their thoughts and actions impact how they feel. Children learn in CBT that avoiding what they fear makes the fear stronger.

They understand that the fear weakens and vanishes when they confront it.

CBT teaches parents how to respond appropriately when their child is worried. They learn how to assist children in confronting their concerns. Children gain coping strategies to tackle fear and concern more effectively.

The therapist assists the children in practicing and provides encouragement and praise as they do so. Kids gradually learn to face their concerns and feel better. They become accustomed to the conditions that they are terrified of. They are pleased with what they have learned. They can talk about other things, such as school, interests, and fun because they do not have as many worries. Medicines are sometimes used to assist manage anxiety.

Healthy habits are crucial for all children, but they are especially vital for children who suffer from sadness or anxiety. In addition to receiving the appropriate medication, a healthy lifestyle can aid in the management of depression or anxiety symptoms.

It is unclear why some youngsters experience anxiety or despair. Many things could be at play. However, it is also recognized that some kids are more likely to acquire anxiety or depression due to trauma or stress, maltreatment, being bullied or abandoned by other kids, or having anxiety or depression in their parents.

Although these characteristics appear to raise the risk of anxiety or depression in youngsters, there are techniques to reduce the likelihood of developing.**Regulate Anxiety Workbook for Kids** is a complete guide to teach your kids to regulate anxiety by using simple, easy, and fun CBT exercises, activities, and games. The book has three chapters. The first chapter is on the thoughts and emotions of kids. The second chapter is on developing positivity in kids. The third chapter is about coping strategies consisting of different mindful and breathing exercises and activities. So why wait? Start reading this book and help your kid with his anxieties before it is too late for you to manage.

WHY CBT?

Cognitive-behavioral therapy works on changing automatic negative thought patterns that can aggravate emotional issues, depression, and anxiety. CBT (cognitive-behavioral therapy) is a type of therapy that educates people how to identify and alter harmful or bothersome thought patterns that influence their behavior and emotions. Unreasonable Detrimental thoughts have a negative effect on one's mood. CBT detects and confronts these thoughts, then substitutes them with more objective, reasonable ones.

1. Benefits of Cognitive Behavioral Therapy

CBT is based on the idea that feelings and thoughts play a significant role in behavior. A person who spends more time worrying about aircraft accidents, runway incidents, and other aviation tragedies, for example, may avoid flying.

Cognitive behavior therapy aims to teach people that, while they may not be able to control every part of their situation, they can influence how they understand and respond to it.

The following are some of the most well-known advantages of CBT:

- It has been demonstrated to be useful in treating a wide range of maladaptive behaviors.
- It is frequently less expensive than other forms of therapy.
- It enables you to adopt healthy thinking habits by recognizing the negative and frequently unrealistic thoughts that stifle your emotions and moods.

- It is a good short-term treatment choice; for example, you can observe results after five to twenty sessions.
- One of the most important advantages of cognitive-behavioral therapy is that it aids in the development of coping skills that may be used now and in the future.
- It is successful both online and in person.
- It is appropriate for people who don't need psychotropic drugs.

2. CBT Techniques

CBT includes more than just identifying thought patterns; it also involves employing a variety of techniques to assist people in overcoming them. Some of the techniques performed includes putting things down, role-playing, calming exercises, and cognitive distractions.

- **Problem-Solving**

Mastering problem-solving abilities can help you determine and resolve challenges that arise as a result of both significant and small life stressors, as well as lessen the negative consequences of mental and physical illness.

Problem-solving in CBT usually consists of five steps:

- The first step is to recognize a problem.
- Compile a list of possible solutions
- Considering the benefits and drawbacks of each viable option
- Selecting a solution to implement
- Execution of the strategy

- **Exercising New Skills**

It is vital to start practicing new abilities in order to use them in real-life situations. For example, an individual with a drug use disorder can start practicing healthy coping strategies and rehearsing techniques to avoid or deal with social situations that could contribute to relapse.

- **Self-Monitoring**

Self-monitoring, often known as diary recording, is an important part of CBT that requires keeping note of your behaviors, feelings, and experiences on a regular basis so that you can discuss them with your psychiatrist. Self-monitoring can assist your psychiatrist in gathering the information needed to give you with the best possible care. For those with eating problems, self-monitoring may involve keeping note of eating behaviors as well as any feelings or sensations associated with that food.

- **Goal-Setting**

Goal setting can aid in the recovery from mental disorder and the implementation of changes to improve your fitness and well-being. During CBT, a therapist can help you build goal-setting skills by teaching you how to define your goal, distinguish between short and the long objectives, create stipulated, measured, attainable, rational, time-based goals, and concentrate on the outcome.

- **Recognizing and Dealing with Negative Emotions**

It is about understanding the role of ideas, emotions, and circumstances in the development of maladaptive behaviors. The technique can be difficult, especially for people who have difficulty with observation, but it can ultimately lead to self-discovery and breakthroughs, which are important in the treatment process.

3. Things to Consider

During cognitive-behavioral therapy, individuals may face several difficulties.

- **Gradual Progress is a frequent thing.**

CBT is a gradual procedure that helps a person change their behavior in little steps in most circumstances. Someone suffering from social anxiety, for example, would begin by visualizing anxiety-inducing social scenarios. They may then begin practicing discussions with friends, family, and strangers. The process appears less overwhelming, and the goals appear easier to achieve by gradually working toward a larger goal.

- **Change can be challenging**.

Some patients first claim that while they are aware that some ideas are not logical or healthful, simply being aware of them does not make it simple to change them.

- **Individuals must be willing to adapt to new situations.**

Individuals must be willing to devote time and effort to evaluate their ideas and feelings for cognitive behavioral therapy to be effective. Although self-analysis and homework can be challenging, they are an excellent way to learn how interior moods influence external action.

- **CBT is well-ordered**

Other treatments, such as psychoanalytic therapy, focus more on fundamental unconscious change resistance than cognitive-behavioral therapy.It is frequently best suited for clients who prefer an organized and concentrated approach in which the therapist frequently acts as an instructor.

4. Effectiveness of CBT

CBT was created in the 1960s as a result of psychiatrists Aaron Beck's findings that certain styles of thinking were associated with emotional problems. Beck invented the phrase "negative automatic thinking" and developed the cognitive therapy method to address them. Rather than focusing almost solely on relationships, punishment, and incentives to modify behavior, the cognitive approach focuses on how thoughts and feelings influence behavior.

Anxiety, hopelessness, binge eating, insomnia, obsessive-compulsive disorders, chronic anxiety, PTSD, and substance use disorder have all been treated using cognitive-behavioral therapy.

CBT has been demonstrated to help those with insomnia as well as those with other physical concerns that keep them awake at night, such as discomfort or mood depression or anxiety. Clinical trials have shown that cognitive-behavioral therapy can help children and teenagers with anxiety and sadness. According to a 2019 meta-analysis of 40 types of study, CBT helped people with anxiety and anxiety-related conditions like eating problems and stress disorders. When it comes to treating substance use problems, CBT has a lot of data to back it up. It can aid in the development of self-control, the avoidance of stressors, and the development of coping mechanisms for stressful situations.

A Letter for Grownups!

We all want to see a happy child, but the easiest method to assist children in overcoming anxiety is not to try to eliminate the stressors that cause it. It is to help them learn to cope with their stress and perform as well as possible, even when they are worried. As a result, anxiety will reduce with time.

It is normal to want to make a child feel better when they are anxious. However, by attempting to shelter children from the things that hurt them, you may unintentionally exacerbate anxiety. The most effective strategy to help children overcome anxiety is to educate them on dealing with it when it arises. They will get less apprehensive with practice.

In the short term, assisting children in avoiding the things they are frightened of can make them feel better, but it will reinforce their worry in the long run. Let's imagine a child is disturbed in an unpleasant scenario and begins to cry — not to be deceptive, but simply because that is how they feel. The youngster has acquired that coping method if their parents take them away or remove the object they are terrified of. And the cycle may repeat.

When a youngster is angry in an unpleasant situation, and their parents remove them from it, the child learns that being unhappy is a useful way to cope.Instead, parents should reassure children that they will be fine, even if they are terrified. You cannot guarantee that nothing bad will happen to your child. You can, however, show confidence that they will be able to face their anxieties and become less fearful with time.

You can exhibit empathy without agreeing with your child's anxieties. "I know you're nervous about getting this injection," you might explain. It is fine to be terrified. You'll be able to get through this, and I'll be there to assist you." Avoiding leading inquiries ("Are you anxious about the exam tomorrow?") is usually good. Ask open-ended inquiries instead, such as "How do you feel about the exam tomorrow?"You may show your child that you are calm by using your manner of facial expressions and body language, which can make them stay calm.

You cannot assure a youngster that their concerns are unfounded—that they won't fail a test, enjoy ice skating, or have another child mock at them during the show and tell. You can, however, show confidence that they will be fine, that they will be able to handle it. You can also tell them that their anxiety will decrease with time when they face their anxieties. This assures them that your expectations are reasonable and that you will not ask them to perform something they are incapable of.

Parents can also assist by keeping children occupied before an upsetting event, such as a doctor's appointment. It can be beneficial to discuss what would happen if their worries came true with your child. What would they do in that situation? Who would they turn to for assistance? Anxiety can be reduced by having a strategy.

Finally, parents may show their children how to cope with anxiety healthily. It is normal for parents to feel apprehensive. The idea is to demonstrate to your youngster that worry is natural and does not have to be a major concern. With the easy and helpful activities in this book, you can help your kids deal with their anxieties and worries in a positive and supportive way.

Bella is an eight-year-old second-grader. Bella has always been a shy child, as per her mother. Her scores have started to decline this year, even though she has generally done well in class. She has also grown unpleasant and introverted. Bella only stays with her two best mates at school, whom she has known since kindergarten. She claims she is terrified of doing anything embarrassing if she hangs around with other girls over lunch or between classes. After one of the popular girls mocked Bella about wearing the "dirty" jeans, she became terrified.Bella also refuses to attend gym class because she does not want to dress in front of other girls and is terrified of making a fool of herself in class. She has skipped two birthday sleepovers due to a tummy ache and refuses to participate in any after-school events or groups. Bella's best friends become irritated since she refuses to do anything with anyone outside of school. Bella claims that she prefers to spend her time with her younger sister. Lastly, Bella's mother has noted that when she's among other kids or people she doesn't know, she has problems with direct eye contact and prefers to mutter and speak quietly.It has been going on for about a year, but it has gotten worse in the last six months.

Dear kids, anxiety is a frequent and typical occurrence that can be successfully addressed! Separating or isolating yourself from others is not the solution. Work hard, overcome your fears and be a brave person. Otherwise, your friendships and relationships will be in danger like Bella, and you will find yourself alone.

Chapter 1: My Thoughts and Emotions

(Read for kids)

Once upon a time, there was a little boy (James) with feelings. James had a lot of emotions, and he expressed them every day. When he expressed his emotions, his family liked him. As a result, he began to wear them on his arms. Then one day, James' father said that he no longer wanted to see James's fear - and he tried to pull it off!

The fear, on the other hand, would not go away! As a result, the father stated that he would give James some difficulties to help him overcome his fear. It was easy to hide the fear under difficulties. Mother and grandmother came to help when James was facing difficulties. It took a long time.When he was in a difficult position, his father said, "Now you look fantastic as you hide (forgot) your fears due to the difficulties." "We have dealt with some of your emotions in a tough way. You will mature into a decent, powerful individual."

When James was a little older, he made a friend. The friend, too, wore his emotions on his sleeve."My mother wants me to mask my lonely sentiments and I'll be different from now on," the friend stated one day. And, indeed, he was!

Jameschose to disguise his loneliness as well. And he was offended by a stranger.

On top of his loneliness, he painted large patches of anger to hide his loneliness. It took a lot of effort to mask the loneliness.

James attended school one day, some of his loneliness began to emerge. As a result, the teacher made him feel guilty about masking his feelings.

When he was alone at night, James would examine his feelings. He would take off the toughness, the wrath, and the guilt and focus on his loneliness and fear. Then he would have to spend a long period re-applying the toughness, wrath, and guilt to hide his other emotions.

One night, he observed that his loneliness and anxiety became more noticeable around the patches.

James had to go out and get angrier to hide the loneliness, and he got all the toughness his father could offer to mask the fear. James increased in height and size. Everyone believed he was good at concealing his emotions.

One day, James' father asked him to show his pride as man are supposed to be strict and tough. However, because the difficulties were getting too big, James couldn't find a spot to show his proud feeling. James struggled to find room on his sleeve for any other emotions.

The toughness and rage were all that was seen. Then one day, James revealed a secret to a friend. "I'm not the same as you... My toughness and rage are just masks for my fear and loneliness."

The friend sat silently and didn't say anything. Then he demonstrated his concern by slowly pulling a small edge of his tough back. And James pushed back a corner of his anger, revealing his loneliness.

The friend then softly caressed James's fear, and then his loneliness - and the friend's touch was magical - because a sensation of acceptance emerged on James's sleeves.And when he took a closer look, he noticed that he was different. His true feelings were on display! And his toughness and rage were reduced!

James realized that he would need to be less difficult whenever someone accepted him. Then he would have more room to express his true feelings...

Whatever they were - joyful, proud, in love, sorrowful, nice, powerful, hurt, good, alone - they were happy, appreciative, sad, pleasant, powerful, hurt, nice, lonely.

Moral of the Story: Every emotion is acceptable as long as your mind and body positively accept them. Parents usually tell kids to hide their emotions while the hidden emotions continuously destroy the kid's present and future. The best things parents can do for their children are to realize that they are normal emotions and a part of everyday life. Consoling your kids by magical touch is what you and your kids need for a stronger bond and happier relationships.

Who Am I?

Instructions: Introducing yourself boosts confidence and enables kids to highlight the unique area of their life. The first activity includes introductory questions. Ask your kid to write the answers, or you can also write by asking your kid. Let them color the shapes.

My Moods Tree

"Mood swings" are a phrase used to describe mood changes. Periods, when the child is too eager and confident are referred to as manic episodes. These emotions can swiftly turn into utter confusion, resentment, and even rage.To help your kids get through their mood swings, I have designed a special mood tree to record their mood changes.

Instructions: Kids will write their mood and what causes that mood in the tree leaves. Big emotions will be written in big leaves and small in smaller ones. Color the tiny leaves.

My Stress Bucket

You should know that the things which do not disturb you can cause stress in children. Don't ignore your children's feelings as wrong by letting them know you understand their worry.While it is not always easy to tell whether a child is stressed, short-term behavioral changes like mood swings, shouting out, changing sleep habits, or bedwetting can all be signs. Some children experience physical symptoms such as stomachaches and diarrhea. Others have difficulty concentrating or finishing their homework. Others retreat or spend quite a bit of time alone.How can you assist children in coping with stress?A stress bucket will help your kids to release their daily stress.

Instructions: Ask kids to writefive things that make them stressed. Let them choose any three. Ask them to write on the arrows above the bucket. The arrows will lead the stress into a bucket, releasing it through the tap. Tell them to color the bucket.

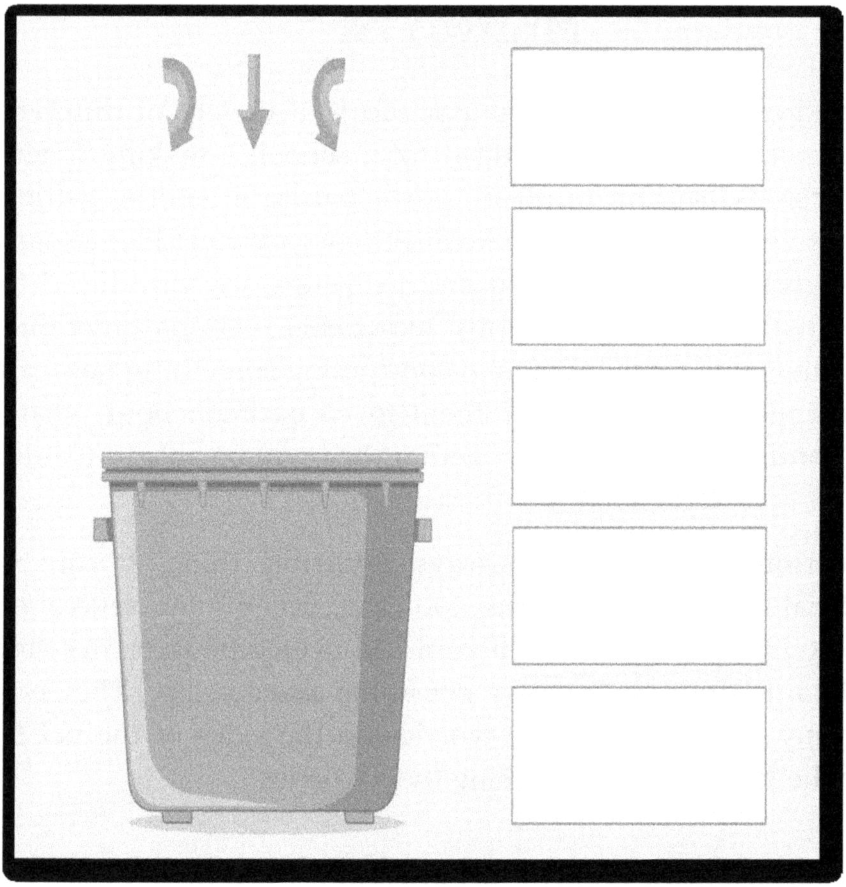

My Worry Pet

As children mature, they are exposed to a variety of different experiences. The first day of school, making new relationships,learning to swim, participating in sports, getting your driver's license,every new experience can feel like a giant leap forward. When children and teenagers are introduced to new situations, they frequently experience various emotions. Even when it is a positive thing, confronting something new can be difficult. It is natural for them to be excited about what's ahead and concerned about whether they will be able to handle it.

Instructions: Worry isnot always a terrible thing. It can be beneficial if it does not persist too long, become too severe, or occur too frequently. To help your kid overcome their worries, ask them to draw their worry pet in the space below. They can draw any pet and write the worries on the sides of the pet to make the pet bigger while losing their worries.

Identifying My Feelings

Feelings can be hard to distinguish at times. Look at your child's body movements, listen to what they are talking about, and observe their behavior to get a sense of their feelings. Knowing what they are experiencing and why they feel it allows you to better assist them in identifying, expressing, and controlling their emotions. Make an effort to comprehend the meaning and emotion behind your child's actions. Give your youngster a label to help them name their emotions. The first step in teaching children to identify feelings is to name them. It enables your child to build an emotional language, allowing them to express their emotions. This feeling activity will help them to identify and name their feelings.

Instructions for Kids: The boy is carrying the threads. You need to draw a balloon with emotion whenever you feel sad, happy, anxious or down etc. I have drawn one for you.

Instructionsfor Table: Write time and day when you were feeling any uncertain emotion. Write the feeling and reason to feel that emotion in the given columns.

TIME/DAY	I AM FEELING

My Mood Bear

These bears do not have a face. Ask kids to make faces of bears by noticing how they are feeling in each situation.

Instructions: Kids will draw the emotions of the bear and missing parts. They will also color them with the shades they want.

Honey

My Fruitful Emotions

Children who can experience pleasant emotions at a young age have more chances to build coping abilities and are more ready to master new skills. A few instances will also be discussed to understand better how positive emotions widen a person's mental and working competencies. The fruitful emotion helps kids to recognize positive emotions.

Instructions: Use these fruits and ask kids to write positive emotions/happy emotions in them. Color the fruits and name them.

Feelings Umbrella

Feelings are part of everyone's life. Having negative feelings most of the time makes kids stressed and worried.

Instructions for kids: Consider that this feeling umbrella is wet with your feelings. Write mostly occurred feelings on the side of umbrella. Connect that feeling with droplets on the umbrella through a line. Forget about that feeling as soon as you write because the droplet will fall soon from the umbrella.

Thoughts, Feelings, Actions Triangle

This picture will assist children and teenagers with comprehending the relationship between emotions, thoughts, and actions, as well as how changing one's thinking can affect one's feelings and actions.

Instructions: Explain this picture to your kids. Thoughts create feelings in kids, and those feelings result in actions. For example, if they think that they are worthless,it will make them worried or anxious. And in response, they will hesitate to do anything new. By learning how their feelings and thoughts affect their daily lives, they will be more aware of their actions.

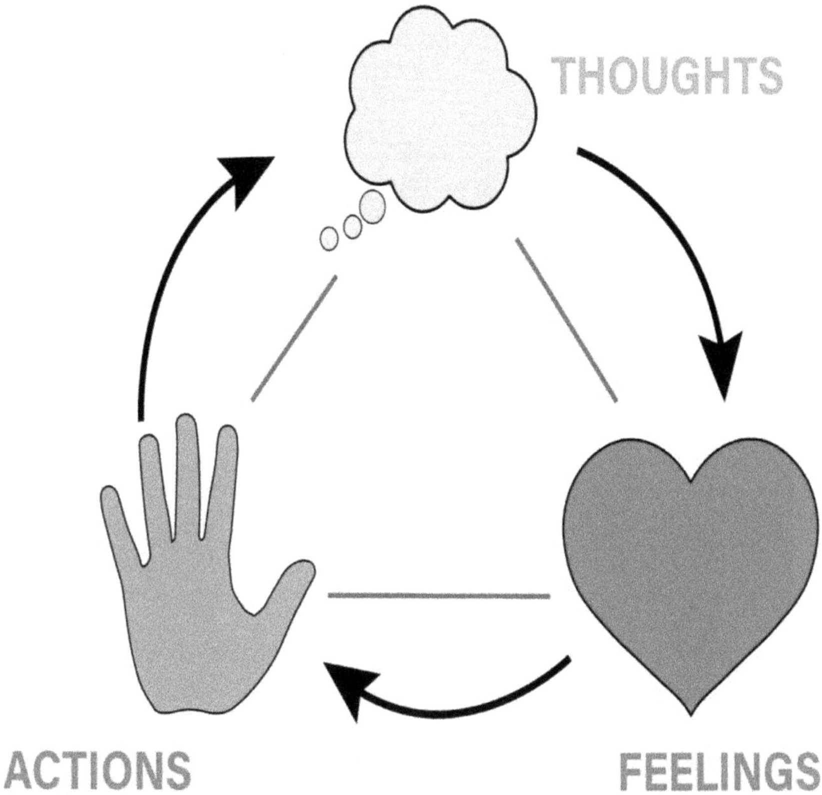

Feeling Angry?

Anger is a healthy and needed emotion sometimes. It can alert children when something isnot right or fair. However, it might become a concern if a child's furious behavior becomes out of control or aggressive. Help your child deal with their anger by working together. In this manner, your youngster understands that the anger is the issue not them. How you react to anger can impact how your child reacts to it. Making it something you and your kids work on together might be beneficial to you. This can be a creative and exciting activity for younger children.

Instructions: help your kid answer the following questions in each box. Tell them to notice their body whenever they feel angry. This way, they will be aware of their body actions and will be able to control them gradually.

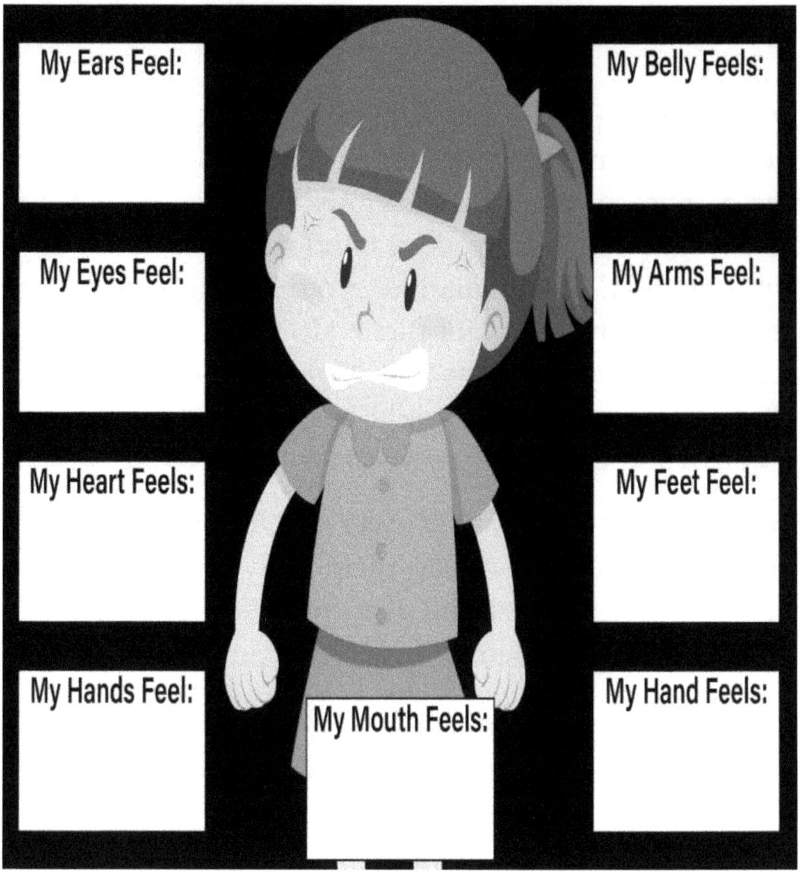
My Ears Feel:
My Belly Feels:
My Eyes Feel:
My Arms Feel:
My Heart Feels:
My Feet Feel:
My Hands Feel:
My Mouth Feels:
My Hand Feels:

Shades of Emotions

When children start to accept and manage their own emotions, they feel happier and may be able to cope better with issues. If they can recognize and talk about them, your child will be less likely to express strong emotions like joy, anger, wrath, or disappointment through problematic behavior like tantrums. Being able to detect and comprehend how others are feeling might also assist your youngster in getting along with others. You can do this activity with your child anywhere and at any time. You just need some colors!

Instructions: Write different emotions in the boxes below. Ask your kids to color each emotion whenever they feel it. Color the sad emotions yellow, happy emotions green, angry emotions red, and other emotions with different colors. Write at the end why they use other colors to describe their emotion.

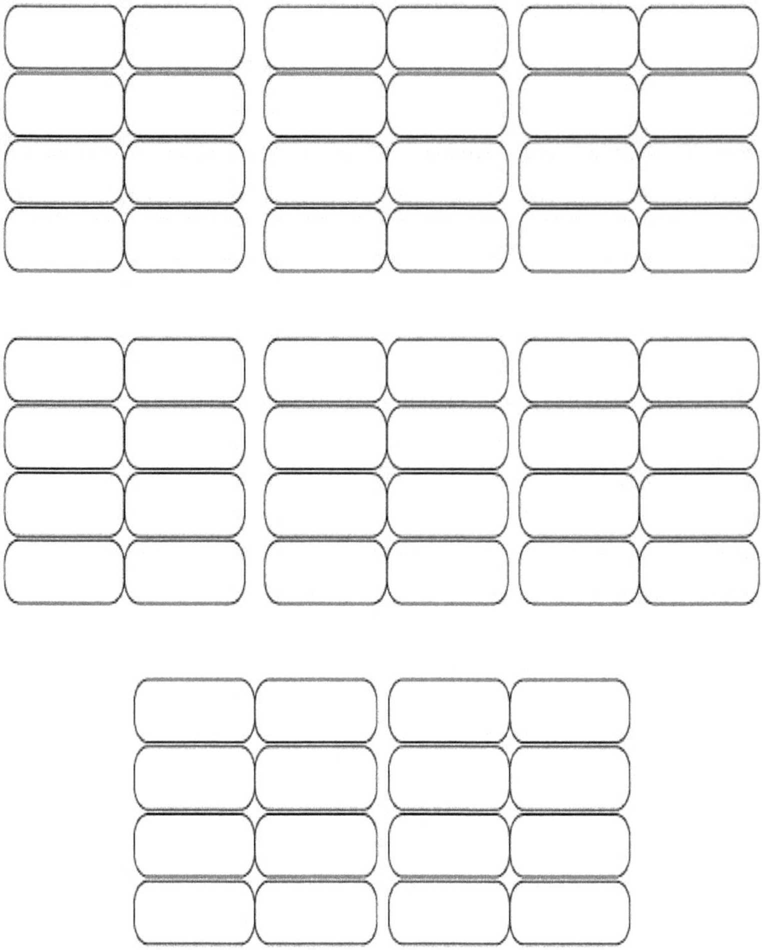

Going from 1 to 5

Moods are part of the day, but it becomes a problem when they change quickly for small reasons or no reason at all. Your kids need to understand the "why" behind the mood swings. To help them recognize these changes, I have designed an easy activity.

Instructions: There are five blanks. Whenever your kid starts feeling angry, ask him to notice his mood. In the first blank (1), write down what was their mood before becoming angry. In other blanks (2, 3, and 4), ask them what the situation was and how they reacted. In the last blank (5), write the current emotion and how they are feeling after being angry. This activity will help them understand their anger triggers.

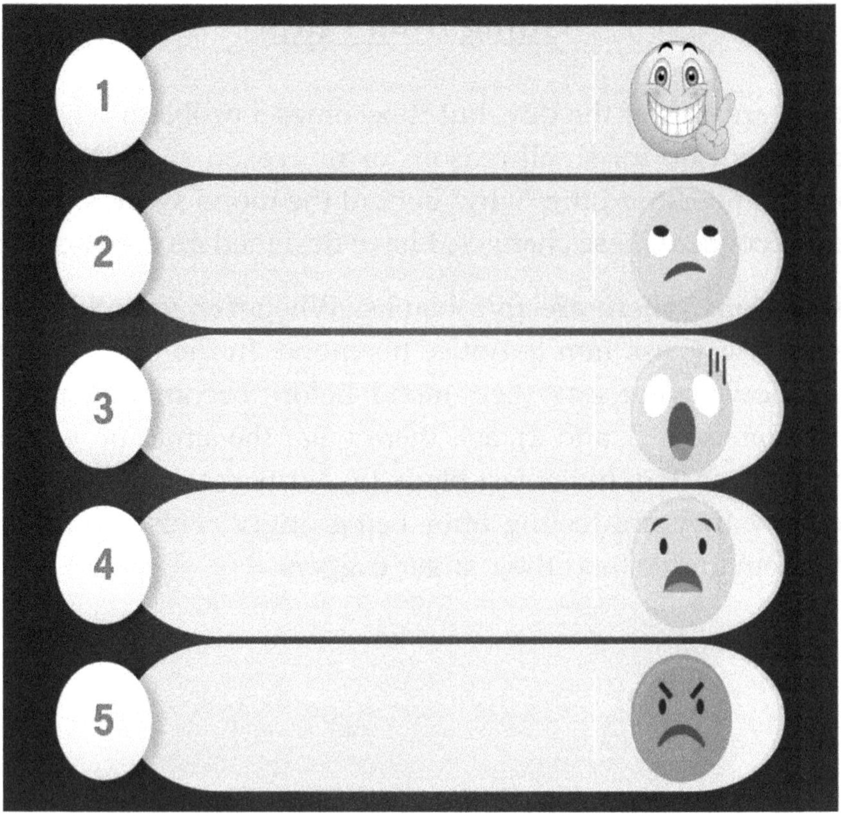
1
2
3
4
5

My Feelings Drawing

Instructions: This is a relaxation coloring activity for kids. Ask them to color this type of picture whenever they feel down or angry. These drawings get the kid's attention, and eventually, they forget about their feelings for the time being.

My Superhero Skills

Superhero skills help kids identify their uniqueness. Recognizing that they are not worthless is the purpose of this activity. As every kid has a superhero, these positive skills will help them to highlight their worth in their life.

Instructions: Ask kids to write down seven superpowers they have, but only they know about them. On the head of the superhero, write the name of the ideal superhero that they want to become. Let them color it to make it similar to their superhero.

My Superhero Skills

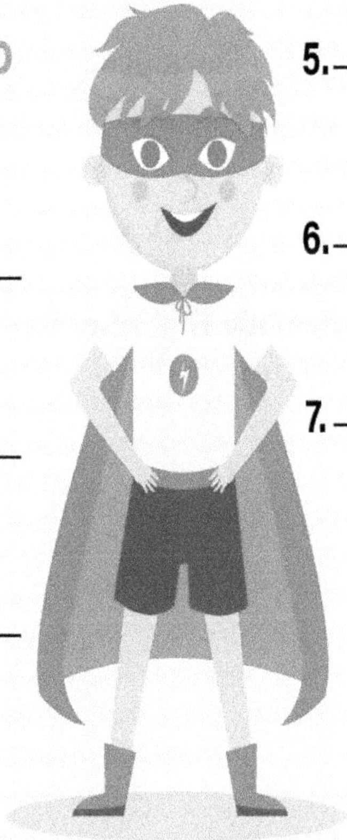

1. ______________
2. ______________
3. ______________
4. ______________
5. ______________
6. ______________
7. ______________

Weekly Emotions Check-In

Recording kids' emotions daily will help you understand their current situation and any progress they have made. There are seven cards with days.

Instructions: Ask kids to look back to the day. Then tell them to draw emotion in a card that dominates the day. Help them to know that the emotions made their day happy or sad according to the emotions they will draw.

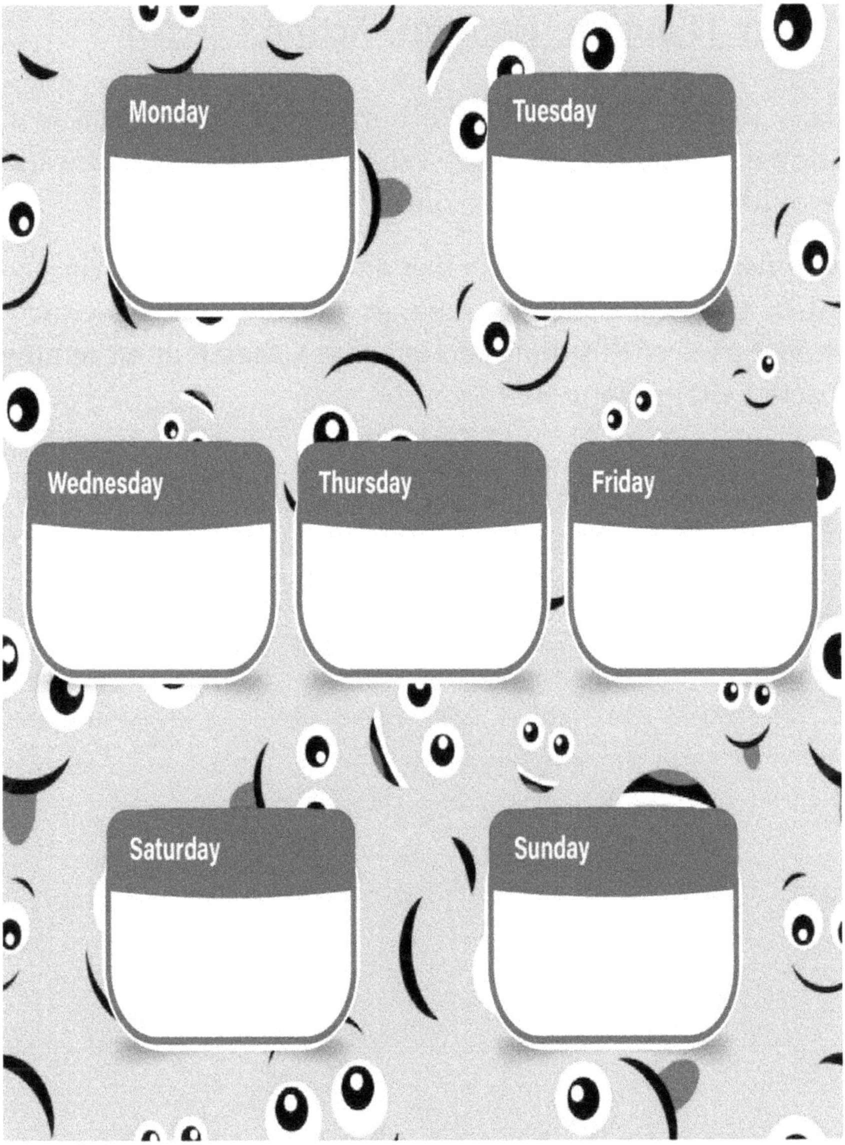
Monday
Tuesday
Wednesday
Thursday
Friday
Saturday
Sunday

My Thoughts, Feelings, Action Journal

This daily journal is for kids. The purpose of this journal is to write down the daily activities. What they thought, felt, and acted would be recorded in this journal.

Instructions: This journal looks like a diary. Kids will write the thought of the day and what feelings that thought generated. On the next page of this diary (action page), they will write how they reacted after getting that thought.

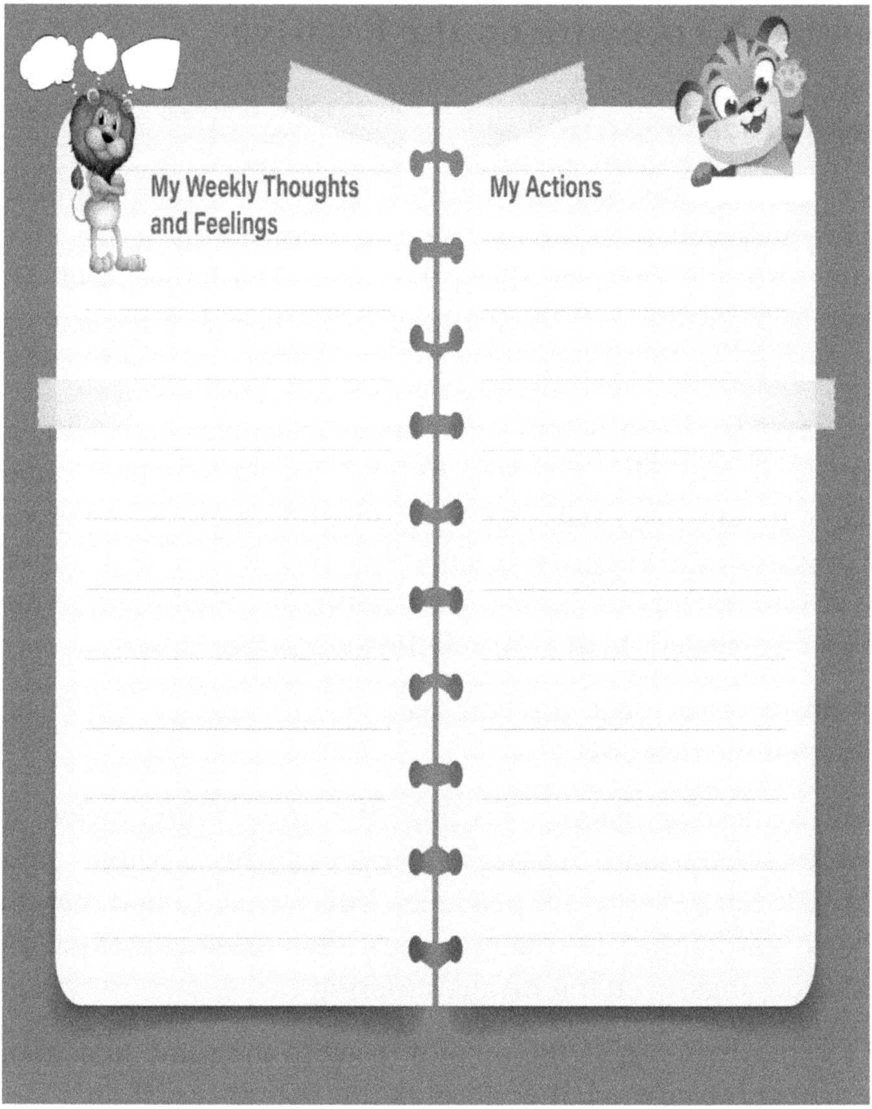
My Weekly Thoughts and Feelings
My Actions

Chapter 2: Focusing on the Positive

(Read for Kids)

There were two disciples for one teacher. One of them seemed to have an excellent positive vision and constantly looked for positive aspects in everything he saw. The other had an unfavorable vision and always looked for negative aspects or flaws in everything he saw.

One day, the instructor and both disciples went to a playground, and while roaming through the garden, they came along a mango tree with some fresh and luscious mangoes growing from it. When the teacher saw this, he decided to put both of his students to the test. As a result, he called them to his side and instructed them to watch the mango tree closely.

"My lovely kid, what do you feel of this mango tree?" he questioned the first one.

"Teacher, despite people beating this tree with rocks, it produces sweet and luscious mangoes," the disciple said quickly. It hurts, yet it still produces fruit for us. I hope that all humans learn from the mango tree's vital message: to share their belongings, even if it means suffering."

The teacher then asked the second disciple the same question, "My dear child, now what you feel of this mango tree?"

"Sir, this mango tree is no great and will only give us fruit if we smash it with stones and sticks," the student responded angrily.As a result, we should strike it hard to get tasty mangoes. The only way to have these mangoes is to do so. It is also obvious from this tree that to receive nice fruits from others, we must first become violent, and only then can we achieve happiness."

The teacher was pleased with the first student's response because he had a commendable vision and praised the positive vision. In contrast, the second student's response displeased him because he saw the tree with deleterious vision and insisted on learning the incorrect method of obtaining fruits in life. He lavished all of his rewards on the first disciple.

So, kids, even if the circumstance is the same, how we interpret it reveals our mental state and how we think about others. Let's look at a beautiful rose with thorns as an example. Someone with a bleak outlook would say, "Oh, my God! Even these lovely blooms have thorns", yet a person with a lucky vision might exclaim, "Wow! What a great natural creation – a lovely rose among the thorns."

Create a vision that can see something positive even in a negative situation or person. And as a result, your mind and intellect will gradually grow pure day by day.

FORM A POSITIVE PERSPECTIVE AND ALWAYS DISCOVER SOMETHING GOOD IN EVERYTHING AND EVERYONE.

Moral of the Story: Positivity is one of life's greatest assets. Those who are positive in all situations are more likely to succeed. Many great superstars had one or more flaws. Still, they were always optimistic about themselves, others, and situations, and as a result, they were able to overcome various challenges. In our minds, a little poisoning of negativity about others can devastate our connections with them. Everyone has something to be grateful for; all we have to do is have a positive outlook and appreciate others.

Keep it Positive

Positive thinking is a mental state that sees things from a positive perspective. Positive thinking principles can be understood by children as early as five years old. As children grow older, they gain a deeper knowledge of positive thinking. Positive thinking is a strong coping strategy that can help a child gain resilience when it is fostered. Parents can instill positive thinking in their children by modeling it in their own lives. Recognize when you are in a bad position or have a bad vibe. Then assist your youngster in seeing things in a positive and productive light. This activity will assist your children in being more positive and productive.

Instructions: He is Jay. Today is his first day in school. He is looking happy.

Let kids write the positive things they can think about by looking at Jay.

I am Thankful

This is a type of gratitude activity. Recognizing positive things and appreciating them in life makes a person worthy. When we indulge in negative thinking, we start ignoring the positivity in our lives. The same happens with kids. When they start feeling worthless, they also start ignoring their positive skills, uniqueness, and many good things that happen with them. This simple activity will assist them to be thankful for the things that they have, and others don't.

Instructions: Kids will write the things they are grateful for, and if they donot have those things, they will lose. Ask them to color as well to make the peacock cheerful.

I AM THANKFUL FOR....

I am afraid of

It is natural for kids to be scared at times. Fear is a powerful emotion that might encourage children to be careful. New, huge, obnoxious, or unusual things can be frightening at first. Parents can assist their children in feeling safe and learning to relax. As children get older, their fears shift. At various ages, certain fears are usual and expected. But some fears cause severe anxieties in kids.

Instructions: Give this worksheet to your kid and ask him to take some time and think about the five things that make him afraid. When they write, help them gradually overcome their fears with some meditation exercises.

I AM AFRAID OF....

1. ____________

2. ____________

3. ____________

4. ____________

5. ____________

Mirror Talk

This is a fun exercise for kids. This exercise aims to make them confident and accept their flaws.

Instructions: Kids will stand up in front of the mirror. Ask them to do the following;

- Look in the eyes for 2 minutes.
- Say something positive about the eyes.
- Look at the smile for 1 minute and tell yourself in the mirror what you feel about your smiley face.
- Look at different body parts and say a positive truth about each.

(Ask them to do this exercise daily and when they are feeling sad or angry.)

MY MIRROR TALK

Self-Love Cards

The self-love cards are part of mirror talk. There are eight cards. Ask kids to fill these cards when they finish their mirror exercise.

Instructions: Write things you like or love about yourself in each card. Write a self-love sentence, draw emotion, and color the card in each card.

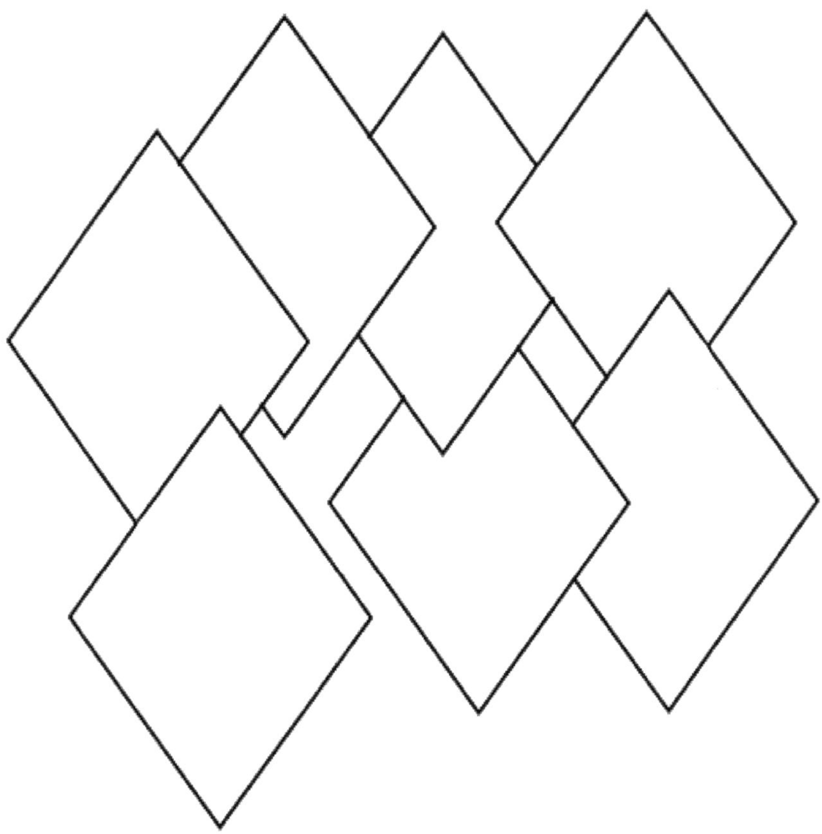

Empathy X-Ray

Kids develop empathy by observing us and seeing our empathy for them. When we empathize with our children, they form safe, trusting bonds with us. Those bonds are crucial to their desire to embrace our values, mirror our behavior, and develop empathy for others. Tuning in to our children's physical needs, understandingtheir different personalities, taking a sincere interest in life are all examples of empathy with our children.You candirect them toward activities that represent what kind of people they are and can do the stuff they enjoy.It is not always because children lack the empathy that they donot express. It is because some emotion or image is preventing them from empathizing. Anger, humiliation, envy, or other negative emotions can often overpower one's ability to care for others. Helping youngsters cope with negative feelings and stereotypical views about others is typically what "releases" empathy in them. This exercise will help them develop their empathy.

Instructions: Ask kids to write what it feels like inside after being kind. Write on the sides of the boy.

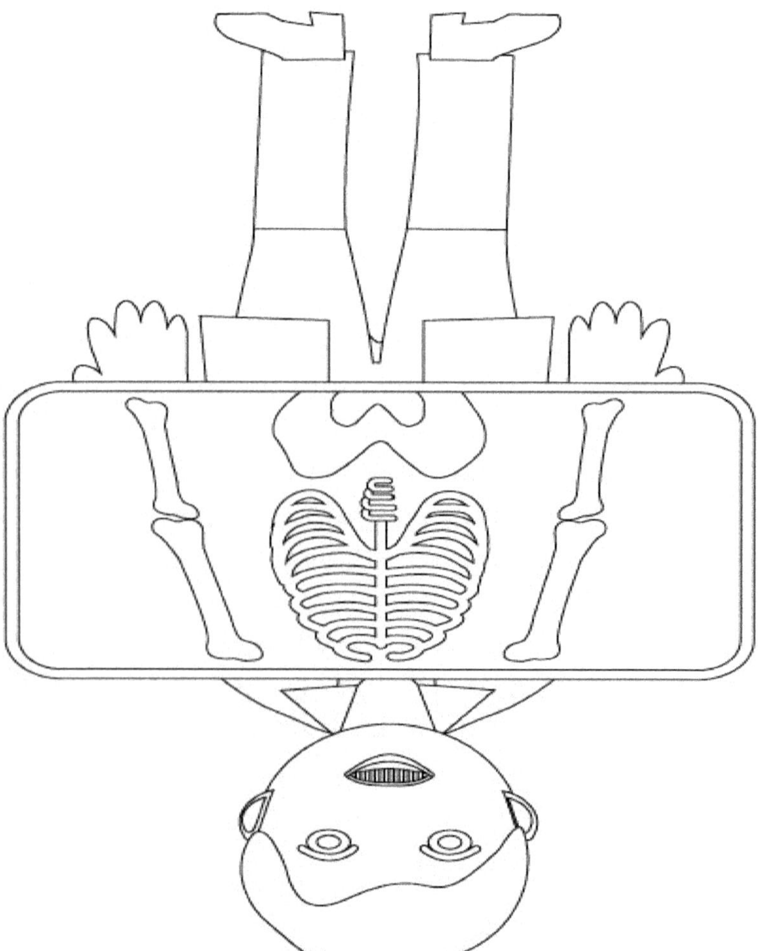

Let it Go

Our capacity to experience pain is one thing that binds us as humans. We have all been wounded somehow, whether it is physical or mental. What distinguishes us, though, is how we deal with the suffering. One of the most effective methods to recover from difficulty is to take the lessons learned and apply them to future growth and progress. We can become paralyzed in terrible sensations and memories if we get stuck thinking about what "could have been." It's critical to concentrate on oneself. You must decide whether or not to face the pain you have felt.The same happens with kids. When they face any embarrassing situation or hurtful event, they keep that into their heart which causes further pain. Learning to let go is a basic life skill. Help your kids to learn this skill through these easy exercises.

What Happened	Did you let it go? Yes/No

Reframing Situations

Sometimes the situation is far different from what we think it will be. For the pain that your kids are causing for themselves by thinking negative situations will not let go easily. You need to tell them that the situation could have another side, the positive side. This activity will help your kids to reframe their minds.

Instructions: Write down the situation, what was your thought. Then at the end of the day, revise the thought and reframe it into a positive one.

What Happened?	Your Negative Thoughts	Reframing into Positive

Daily Affirmations

It is more crucial than ever to encourage your child's emotional development. Positive affirmations are remarks that are motivating and encouraging. Positive affirmations can come from others, such as parents or instructors, and children can learn to apply them in their self-talk.

Self-affirming affirmations are a sort of positive self-talk that may be done anywhere and at any time.

Affirmations for children usually consist of short scripted lines that are either generic or customized to a certain activity. When faced with difficulty, a child battling anxiety would say something positive like "I can accomplish hard things," but a youngster dealing with anger might say, "I can stay cool and in control."

The words we send ourselves have a big impact on our pleasure, productivity, and general health. They have an impact on how we feel about ourselves and the world.

Children with a positive view are often happier and better able to cope with stress. Affirmations assist fight invasive bad emotions and those annoying Automatic Negative Thoughts and increase self-esteem and foster a growth mentality. This affirmation activity is a tool for your kids to be more confident in their lives.

Instructions for Kids: Look at the flower below. The flower has many petals. Write an affirmation sentence you receive in each petal and color to make it look beautiful and cheerful.

My Thoughts and Choices

Negative thoughts affect the decision-making in kids. They make choices by thinking only negative perspectives of the situation. This activity aims to help kids understand that their thoughts can have a huge impact on their choices and eventually on their lives.

Instructions: Kids will think of some situation or event. Ask them to write any thoughts regarding that situation. Then tell them to write the choice they made while being affected or not affected by the thought. For example, the instructor asked the kid to present in class because of his good English. The kids thought that other kids would make fun of him, so he chose to reject the opportunity to present in the class.

My Thoughts	My Choices

My Holiday Fun

It is a fun exercise that will help you observe how your kid feels and does or wants to do on his holidays. Do the things they want to with them so that you both can have a stronger bond.

Instructions: Write the day and date of the holiday. Write what you did during your holiday. Then write what you want to do that can make your holiday fun.

Holiday	What I did	What I Wanted to Do

I Can Do Vs. I Cannot Do

Accepting the good and bad things is necessary, but accepting the things that your kid can do or cannot do is also important to know. This exercise will help you with how your kids consider themselves and which things they are having difficulty with.

Instructions: Ask kids to write what they can and cannot do. Then help them understand that nothing is impossible with hard work and a clear goal.

I Can Do	I Cannot Do

My Good Habits

Everyone wants that their kids grow up with positive and good habits. This good habit exercise will assist you in developing those habits in your kids.

Instructions: Kids will mark the day with a tick mark before each activity after accomplishing it. Encourage them to do each activity daily. Reward them when they complete a day with all ticks.

My Good Habits	Sunday	Monday	Tuesday	Wednesday	Thursday	Friday	Saturday
I brushed my teeth							
I took a warm bath							
I did some exercise							
I helped someone							
I did positive							

thinking.							
I watched my favorite cartoons.							
I ate healthy food							

My Worry Thoughts Vs. My Happy Thoughts

Instructions: Ask kids to write their daily thoughts. Happy thoughts in the left column and worry thoughts in the right column. Then analyze how worried thoughts changed the emotions and how happy thoughts made the day. Here is an example for you.

WORRY THOUGHTS		HAPPY THOUGHTS
"I DON'T KNOW WHAT THE RULES ARE"	→	"MY NEW TEACHER WILL GO OVER ALL THE NEW RULES
"I DON'T KNOW ANYONE ON THE BUS"	→	"I AM GOOD AT MAKING NEW FRIENDS"
"MY TEACHER WON'T LIKE ME"	→	"HE IS ON MY SIDE AND WILL LOOK OUT FOR ME"
"I AM SCARED"	→	"I AM BRAVE"

Now, it's your turn.

In or Out of Control

Everyone cannot do everything. Some things are not always in our control. But what we can control is our thoughts, feelings, and actions related to those thoughts. I have an easy activity for your kids to understand what they can control about themselves and what they cannot.

Instructions for kids: Here you have a superman. This is you. If you are this superman, what will you do first? With the superman powers, what you want to control that you cannot control now. Write the things you can control on the face side of superman. Write the things that you cannot control on the backside of superman.

Love Languages

The first step in determining your child's major love language is to observe how he expresses his affection for you. Why? We all tend to give affection the way we like to receive it. But when we grow older, we learn that the golden rule of giving the love same as we receive is no more applicable.The reason is that we need to love others in the best way for them. But, most children aren't aware of this, they respond with the type of affection they desire. Your child's request is the final part of the puzzle of love languages. This exercise will explore the internal love languages of your kids.

Instructions: There are some pictures below. Ask kids to write down a story in front of the picture they can think of by looking at it. Ask them to write the type of love they want to receive by observing that picture.

7-Day Positivity Challenge

This is a weekly goal-setting exercise. The goal must be related to bringing positivity in life.

Instructions: Ask kids to set a target for each day. Then make them work on the target and mark if they have achieved it or not. Reward them whenever they achieve a goal and if they fail to achieve, motivate them through some appreciation.

Days	My Positivity Target	Achieved or not?
Monday		
Tuesday		
Wednesday		
Thursday		
Friday		
Saturday		
Sunday		

Chapter 3: Coping Skills Package

To understand why coping skills are necessary to learn, I have a story of Ben, an anxiety patient who suffered a lot in his life just because he did not seek help and was struggling alone with his situations.

Hello kids. I am Ben. Emotions are extremely powerful and should be appreciated rather than ignored. This was a hard lesson for me to learn.

Instead of dealing with my problems, when someone hurt me, I reverted to personal attacks.

I was put in a group home when I was in junior high. I had no idea why I had been taken away from my parents. I only knew that being away from my family made me feel extremely lonely and abandoned. I had the impression that I was the last human on the earth.

There were few individuals to turn to in the group home and little room to express my feelings.In the home, there were bad boys bullying others. I was in a lot of pain, but I couldn't tell anyone because I didn't want to be labeled a crybaby. I was well aware that being helpless was not a smart option. As I was just a small kid, so, whenever someone used to attack me, I always tolerated it.

Girls were the only ones who paid attention to what I said and reacted to it. However, by my junior year, I had discovered that no female, at least in my junior high, wanted to be with a gloomy and emotional person. As a result, when I was 14 years old, I transformed my persona.

I took on the role of "bad boy." I skipped class since I was dressed poorly. I used to be emotional and worried about other people's feelings. But now that I was the bad guy, I had to hide my actual self. I feigned not to care when I found out that an ex-girlfriend had cheated on me. My previous self would have wept, grumbled, and done anything to reclaim her. But now, whenever I had the opportunity, I would show her how pleased I had been without her so she would see she had made a bad decision. I wanted her to think that her actions had no negative consequences for me. I was fine as long as I didn't come across as a weak person to others.

I got better at masking my feelings as I grew older. Instead of dealing with my problems like an adult, when someone hurt me, I reverted to character insults. I was pretty skilled at reading people, so I knew exactly what to say to make them feel bad. I was snarky, and I learned to ignore how my remarks affected others.

Things had gotten to the point that I was contemplating suicide. There were too many things going on in my life. I desired to be free of the suffering I was experiencing. I thought the pain I was experiencing was worse than death and I had a severe panic attack.

After reaching such a low place, being in the hospital was a wake-up call. I stayed for three days there. Several other patients shared their stories with me around that time, encouraging me to make a genuine effort to improve. They also advised me to keep in mind one thing: change takes time. It could take months for some and years for others. I began to feel a glimmer of hope as well. To avoid returning to my lowest point, I told myself that I would begin seeing a therapist.

So, kids, being coward, anxious, nervous, stressed or having suicidal thoughtsare not the only options you have. If I had sought help from a therapist earlier in my childhood, I could save my years of being foolish. I could save my relations. You can still change your life as you have a lot of things to do with your friends and family. Work hard, give some time to your thoughts and use these coping skills to make your life as fulfilling as I am having now.

My 5 Fingers Strategy

This is a fun and entertaining exercise to see how your kids react in a certain situation by using their coping strategy.

Instructions: Ask kids to write down five common strategies they use to get through a certain situation. Help them to set better-coping strategies and guide them.

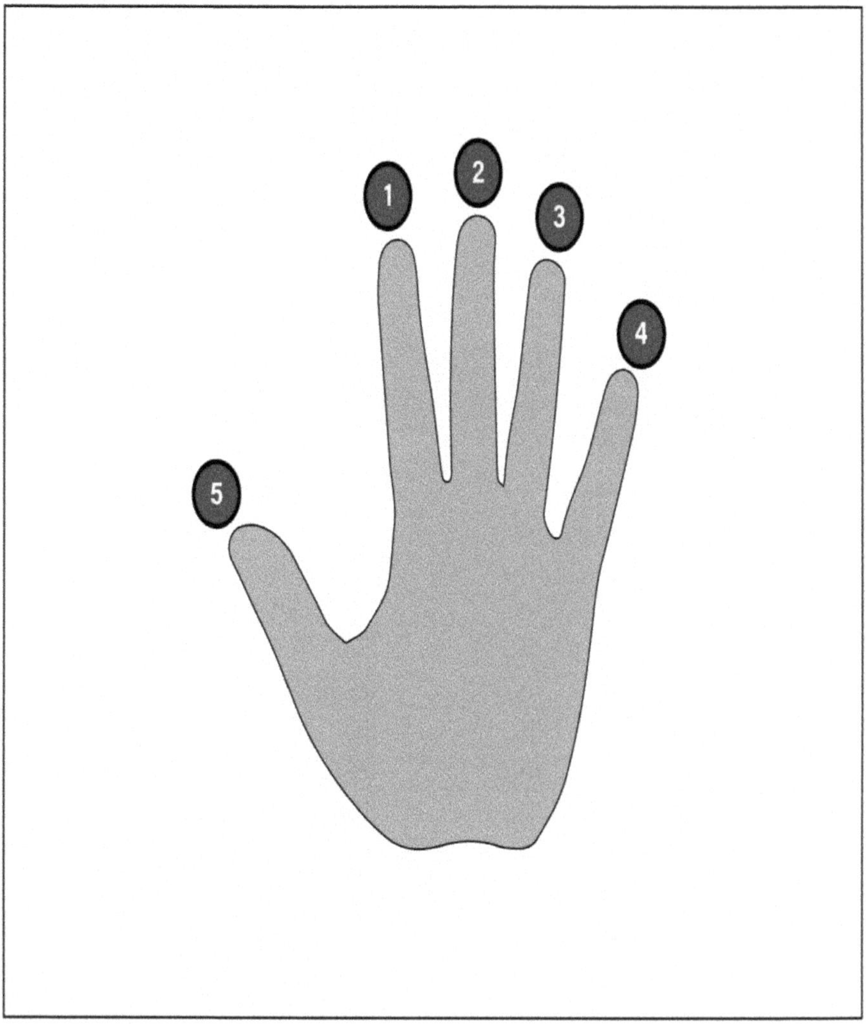

My Coping Skills Wheel

A coping strategies wheel is a useful tool for teaching stress management coping methods. We frequently believe that children know how to relax when they do not! That is why specifically teaching relaxing practices can be quite beneficial.

A coping strategies wheel is a spinning craft that exposes various coping skills from which children can choose. Kids can also create their personalized wheel with tactics customized to their needs. This encourages children to "buy-in" to coping strategies by allowing them to choose which ones they wish to practice. Children can spin and practice the strategies after completing the craft. When the kid or young adult is angry later, they can use the wheels to remind them of which coping skills to employ to help them regain their calmness.

Instructions: Kids will write their most commonly used coping strategies on the wheel. Cut the wheel or make a wheel similar to the given one. Paste it on a cardboard or hard chart. Whenever kids have a stressful time, they will spin the wheel, and the wheel will select the strategy to calm down at the moment.

MY COPING SKILLS
WHEEL

All Feelings are OK

Instructions: Feelings are all normal and OK for everyone. With this activity, ask kids to write down a certain feeling your kid can notice with each picture and write on the side. Make them recognize their feelings and help them to accept them as part of everyday life.

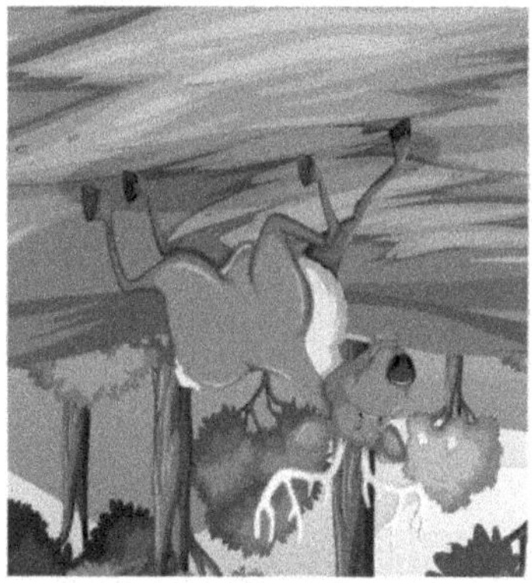
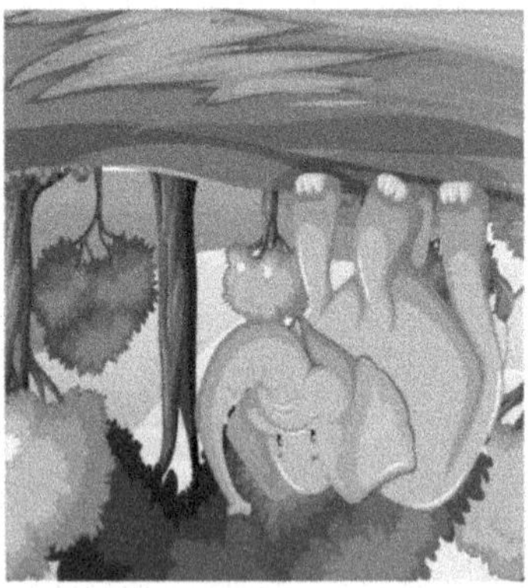

My Calmness Toolbox

It is a creative exercise for kids to make their calmness toolbox.

Instructions: Below, I have given some space. Ask kids to prepare their calmness toolbox. Paste it in the space below and use it when they need to calm down. For example, the calmness toolbox could have some games, some music suggestions, exercises, activities, cartoon series, or anything they enjoy doing the most.

First Aid for Feelings

Instructions: Ask kids to draw their first aid box in the space given below. It can include some games, activities, things they like to do, exercises, and anything that heals them and works as their first aid.

Returning from 5 to 1

In the activity "Going from 1 to 5," kids have understood the triggers, and their emotions change. In this returning activity, they will learn what can make them normal and help in returning to their previous mood.

Instructions: Ask kids to notice and write what made them angry. Then ask them to notice how much time they took to come to a happier mood and what were the reasons for 2, 3, and 4 moods. Help them to understand positive emotions.

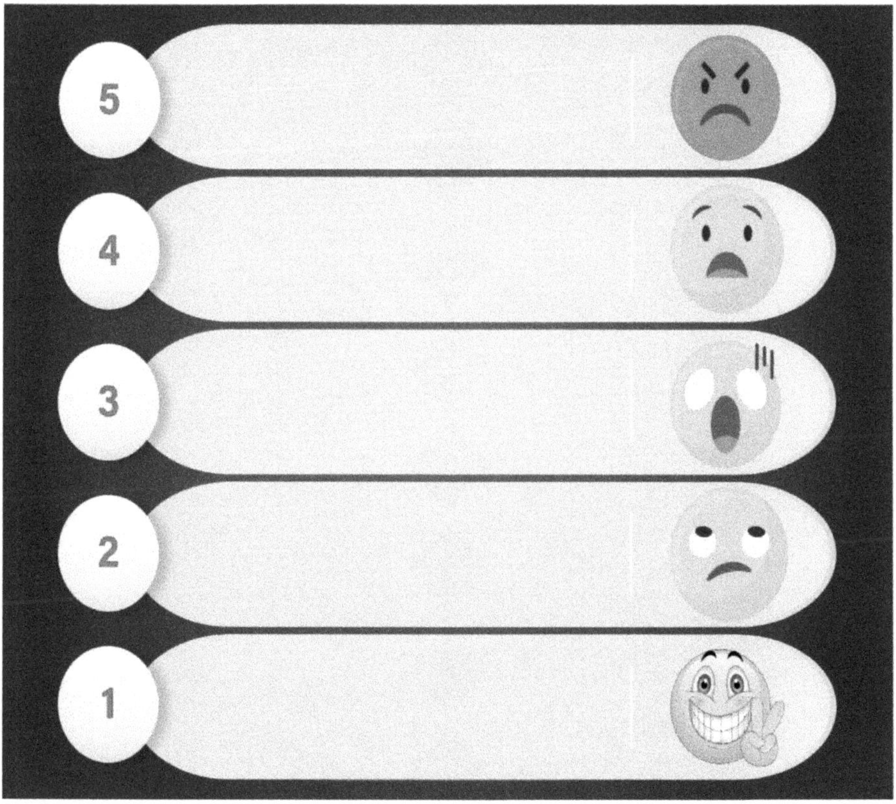

I am Brave

This activity is to boost the confidence of your kids. This brave exercise will explore the secrets and skills of your kids positively.

Instructions: Ask kids to write down the things they can do to make them feel brave. Then in the next column, ask them to write the things they want to do to become brave in the style they desire to be.

How much BRAVE I am	The way I want to be BRAVE

Decode Angry Feelings

Hey kids, don't get bored. I have a fun game for you. It is a coding game. Use the codes in the picture and find the feelings.

7 18 21 13 16 25 =

6 21 19 9 15 21 19 =

1 14 7 18 25 =

1 14 14 15 25 5 4 =

6 18 21 19 20 18 1 20 5 4 =

1	=	A	14	N
2	=	B	15	O
3	=	C	16	P
4	=	D	17	Q
5	=	E	18	R
6	=	F	19	S
7	=	G	20	T
8	=	H	21	U
9	=	I	22	V
10	=	J	23	W
11	=	K	24	X
12	=	L	25	Y
13	=	M	26	Z

Deep Breathing

Breathing is an essential activity that most of us are unaware of. The mere process of inhaling and exhaling, on the other hand, can have a significant impact on our emotions and ideas. Deep breathing has historically been utilized as a relaxation method, and it is beneficial to both adults and children. Breathing exercises can assist children in taking deep breaths in a variety of ways.

To teach and practice deep belly breath with the child, follow these steps:

1. Ask your youngster to take a few deep breaths and assess how they're feeling.
2. Place one hand on your child's tummy (just above the lower abdomen) and the other on their chest area.
3. Instruct your kid to breathe deeply through their nostrils, fill their lungs with air, and push it down towards their stomach.
4. Notice how their bottom hand rises as their tummy swells up and out.
5. Then tell your child to softly exhale through their nose, letting the bottom hand return to its original position.
6. You can instruct your child to try to blow out candles, keep their palm over their lips to feel their breath, or even make a sound with their exhale to promote a slow exhale.
7. Encourage your child how to think and if they notice any changes after taking several deep belly breaths.
8. Ask your child to focus on bringing the air further into their abdomen if their hand on their breast is the only hand going up and down while they breathe.

Star Breathing

Have you ever instructed a kid to breathe deeply, but any of them begin panicking? Or do they inhale but do not exhale?

Kids may require more assistance in learning how to take a deep breath correctly.

Calming exercises are aimed to support your child's transition from "fight, flight, or freeze" state to "relax and digesting" mode. Deep breathing allows more oxygen to enter the bloodstream by widening capillaries. It has a physiologic effect on the body that helps to relax and reduce tension.

I've included a picture to help your child comprehend star breathing. To begin star breathing, assist them following the sides of stars as shown in the image.

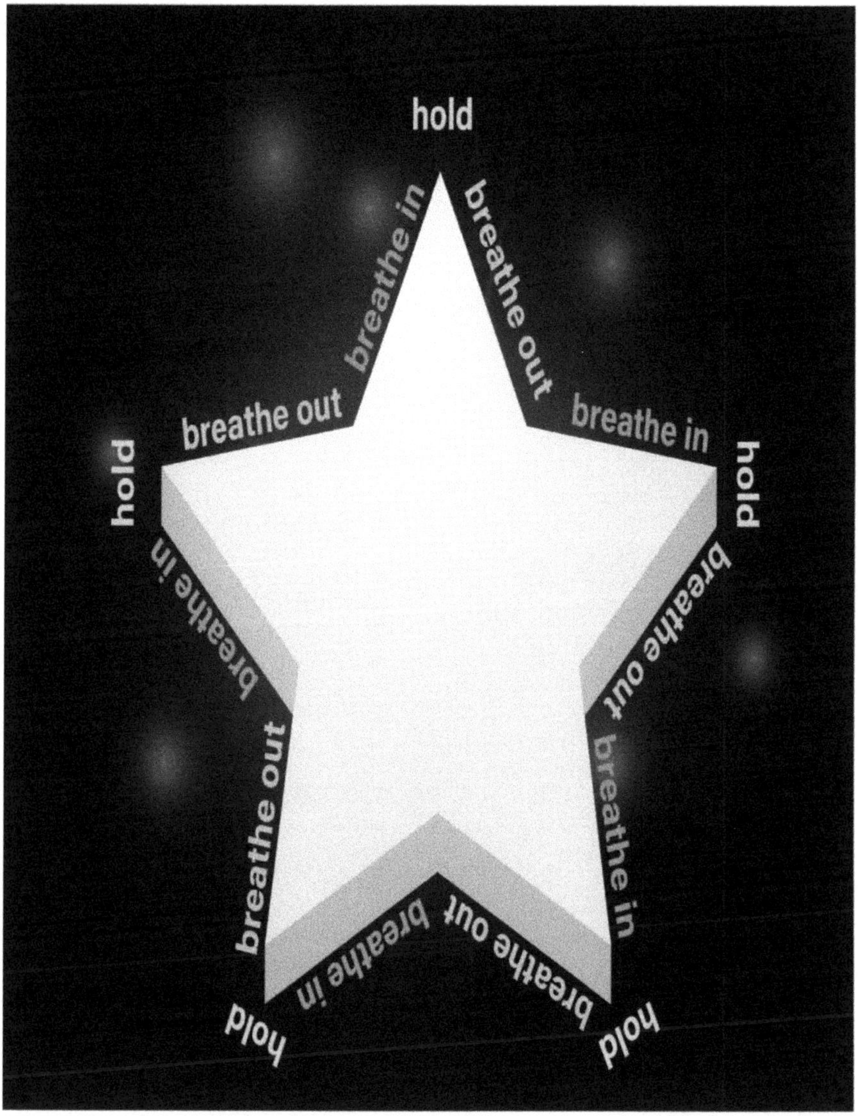

Instructions for Kids

1. Begin on either of the star's "Breathe in" sides.
2. Run your fingers over the point's "breathe in" side.
3. When your finger reaches the tip of the point, pause your breath.

4. Exhale as you trail your finger along the point's other side.
5. Continue till you reach your starting point.
6. You will have taken Five deep breaths once you have traced the entire star.

Butterfly Breathing

Your kid is angry, and things are getting out of hand. Alternatively, you may be aware that your child is worried and are unsure how to help them feel better. I'd like to offer an easy, entertaining technique for kids. The following is how it works:

1. Let your child know that there is something you can do to help them feel better. It is usually ideal for assisting your kid while his or her emotions havenot reached a breaking point. It is best if you can help as quickly as possible.
2. Request your kid to play the role of a butterfly! Demonstrate how butterfly wings should seem to your child. Hold your arms out in front of you and bring them together. Then fly out again, flapping your arms and wings.
3. Observe how your child's butterfly wings function together. Practice is always beneficial in terms of being able to recall information when it is needed.
4. Allow your child to watch the butterfly flap its wings and breathe. Show your child how to breathe like a butterfly. This can be accomplished in a variety of ways. The most crucial message to the butterfly is to take a big breath. Showing and speaking through the following wing/breathing rhythm is one approach to model this.
5. Take a deep breath as the butterfly expands its wings - you can repeat 1, 2, 3 as you spread your wings.
6. Let the breath out and all your anxieties out as the butterfly shuts its wings - you can repeat 3, 2, 1 as you lock your wings.

7. Repeat "Butterfly Breathing" until your kid is calmer as kids learn this method, model it for them, and execute it with them.

Guided Imagery

Guided imagery is a simple yet effective practice with numerous physical and mental health advantages. It can help us feel less scared or angry, suffer less pain, or attain a goal like sports or academic success. You can train to use your imagination to "generate the state you desire" through guided imagery, which means you can modify how you feel and what you focus on. Even small kids can master this talent by associating mental images with feelings and events. This activity teaches kids about the detrimental effects of tension and stress and how to relax using guided imagery.

Before starting the exercise, use an elastic band to demonstrate it to kids how being stretched and strained too much or too long may affect us. Stretch the elastic as far as it will go, emphasizing that if we hold it in this position for too long, it will crack. Explain that the same is true for humans; to be healthy, we must be able to relax, quiet down, and release our tension.

Explain guided imagery by describing it as a technique for creating mental images that can help you feel peaceful and relaxed. Then take them via this straightforward guided imagery exercise.

Instructions for Kids

- Take a seat in a position that is comfortable for you. You have the option of sitting or lying down. Take note of how you are currently feeling in your body and mind.
- Inhale deeply through your nose and exhale slowly from your mouth.
- Breathe deeply, and exhale, notice how your entire body relaxes.

- Continue to take calm, gentle breaths.
- Breathe in relaxation.... and exhale any anxieties... Breathe in calmness.... and let go of all your worries as you exhale...
- Now imagine an environment where you are completely at ease and satisfied. This could be a beloved place you have visited or a location you have seen, or it could be completely made up. It is entirely up to you.
- Imagine yourself in a cheerful, peaceful environment.

Now is the time to start filling in the blanks: What do you see there? How does this fantastic, serene, favorite spot smell?

- Assume how your body is feeling. You are at ease, enjoying the pleasant weather.... satisfied to be still and calm or to engage in any fun activities you choose here.
- Enjoy how you feel in this secure environment.
- You are at ease and secure here.
- Take note of the surroundings in this location once more.
- Take a few seconds just to be here and enjoy everything. It will soon be time to depart, but remember that you can return here in your thoughts at any time to relax, feel relaxed, and feel secure.
- Parents will count to four in a moment. On the count of four, you can feel more aware and energized.
- One, take a long, cleansing breath in... and gently exhale.
- Two... take another big breath... and exhale...
- Three.... you are relaxed, confident, and revitalized.
- Four…. Rest and enjoy the surrounding for some time.

Backward Counting

Backward counting is an exercise to help kids deal with their mood changes. Whenever your kids have a bad day or a mood swing, ask them to read backward counting starting from 50 to 1 loudly.

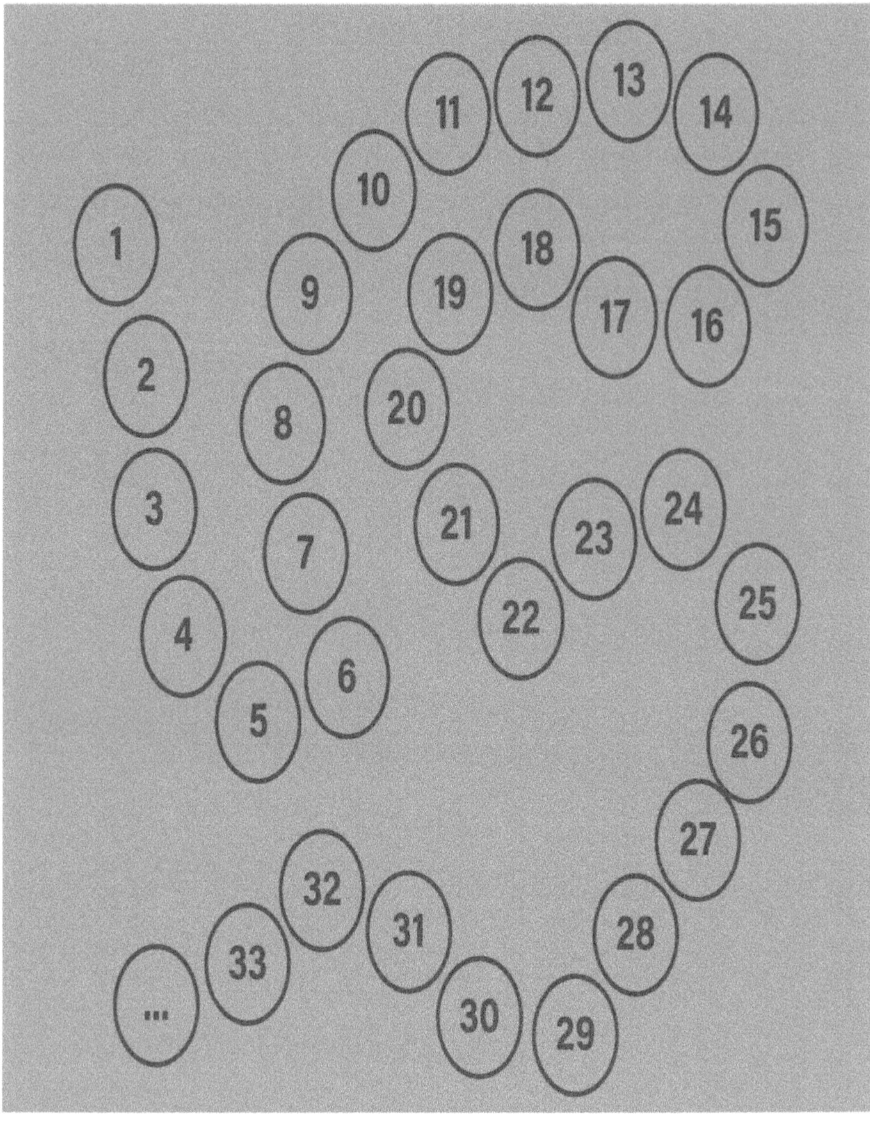
1
2
3
4
5
6
7
8
9
10
11
12
13
14
15
16
17
18
19
20
21
22
23
24
25
26
27
28
29
30
31
32
33
...

Coping Skills Bingo

Coping skills bingo is a fun game you can play with your kids.

Instructions: Give your kids 5 to 10 minutes to write down emotions as much as they can think about. Help them to fill the table. Sit far from each other and play the same as playing a bingo game (calling emotions one by one and drawing straight lines). One who will draw the five straight lines first will win the game.

Mindful Morning Routine

Scheduling the mindful morning routine is not difficult. You need to start with some mindful exercises videos to help learn your kid faster the mindful techniques.

Instructions: Help your kids choose seven mindful techniques for each day of the week. Start the morning with a mindful exercise. Ask them to writein the given table the technique they used, their experience, and how the whole day was spent due to mindfulness.

Mornings	Mindful Technique I Used
Sunday Morning	
Monday Morning	
Tuesday Morning	
Wednesday Morning	
Thursday Morning	

Friday Morning	
Saturday Morning	

My Coping Strategies Notebook

This notebook is for daily check-in about the coping strategies that your youngster used for his fears, anxieties, worries, and stress.

Instructions: Guide your kid to notice their thoughts or feelings in the morning, afternoon, and evening. Then ask them to think about what they did when they had the thought and feelings. For example, the thought could be, "I should not go for a walk today because I want more sleep." For coping strategy, they will gather courage and think of their better health and decide to go for a walk.

My Strateg ies	Mon day	Tues day	Wednes day	Thurs day	Frid ay	Satu rday	Sun day
Morni ng							
Aftern oon							

Evenin g							
Night							

Chapter 4: Dealing with Anxiety: Strategies

When children have worried thoughts, grownups in their lives frequently intervene to remedy the problem.

Is not it sensible to keep kids away from the Pit bull next door if theyare afraid of dogs?

No, not at all. You are supporting and fueling their worry by assisting them in avoiding scary situations. They are also missing out on chances to practice coping techniques and prove that they can handle the worrying thought or feeling the next time it arises. Helping your child learn to manage anxiety is the finest thing you can do for them.

How you react to your child's worry will significantly impact how they develop to cope with anxiety.

Validate Their Feelings

It is easy to say things like, "Oh, it's not a big issue," or "Don't stress about it," when your child expresses concern about something. “You're going to be OK." Such reactions provide the message that your child's emotions are incorrect.

Instead, confirm their feelings by saying something like, "It seems like you are nervous right now," or "I'd be anxious too if I had to speak in front of a large crowd."

Then, despite their anxiousness, write a message expressing your confidence in their ability to achieve. "It's difficult to undertake scary things like this," and then add, "but I am sure you can do it."

Tackle Negative Thoughts

Your child, like adults, is vulnerable to negative thinking. This kind of negative thinking can make them feel anxious and lower their self-esteem.

You may educate them on identifying bad emotions, challenging them, and using positive self-talk to convert them into happy, realistic ones.

- Embrace it. They must first be able to recognize a negative idea before they may address it. Assist them in making a shortlist of unpleasant thoughts that they frequently have.
- Put it to the test. Encourage your youngster to think of themselves as a detective, gathering evidence to evaluate the evidence behind their worrisome thoughts. For instance, if they often tell themselves, "Is it true that I'm stupid?" they should observe themselves for the time being and then again ask themselves,"Am I an idiot? Have there been moments when I've demonstrated my intelligence?" It will teach them not to believe every bad thought that enters their minds.
- It should be corrected. The final phase is to replace their negative self-talk with a positive one after recognizing and challenging it. "Oh dear, you are not stupid," donot say straight away. They will not only refuse to trust you, but they will also refuse to learn how to change their anxious thoughts. "What would you say to a colleague who believed they were stupid?" instead. Urge them to tell themselves the same thing when they respond with kindness.

I CAN'T
...
OH NO!
IMPOSSIBLE

Real Threats and False Alarms

Discuss with your kid how anxiety serves to keep them safe. For example, if a tiger were hunting them, their brain would send a warning signal to their body. They might experience physical changes such as sweaty palms and a faster heart rate. As they were ready to run from the tiger, they would feel a surge of energy (a real threat).

Then inform them that their brain can also set up a false warning at times. They may experience great panic due to these false alarms, even if the scenario isnot life-or-death. Examples of false alarms are situations such as trying out for the basketball game, speaking in front of a large group, or preparing for a huge test. Explain that if there is a serious threat, they should pay attention to the warning signs and take steps to protect themselves. If it is a false alarm, though, confronting their anxieties is good.

The Stepladder Approach

Anxious children will frequently go to great efforts to avoid their anxieties. Unfortunately, avoiding them simply makes them more anxious. Although it may be frightening at first, confronting anxieties will help you overcome anxiety in the long term.

If your child is scared of something specific, such as sleeping alone in the dark or making new friends, use the stepladder approach to help them face their anxieties one small step at a time. The idea of this strategy is for them to perform something reasonably scary—and then practice it until it becomes less scary. They can then proceed to the next level.

Make a list with your child of the actions they can take to tackle their fears and achieve their overall objective. If your child has been sleeping in your bed, here's an idea of how you might assist them in overcoming their fear of sleeping alone:

1. Place a mattress on the floor next to your bed for your child to sleep on.
2. Allow your child to sleep on the floor, but put it closer to the middle and away from the bed.
3. Allow your child to sleep on a mat on the floor in the room, understanding that you will place them in their bed after they fall asleep.
4. Allow your child to fall asleep in their room with you present.
5. Allow your child to fall asleep in their room with the understanding that you will monitor them every few minutes until they fall asleep.

6. Allow your youngster to fall asleep with the light on in their room.
7. Allow your youngster to sleep with only a nightlight in their room.

You might give your child a special privilege or incentive if they reach a certain milestone. Natural repercussions can also be used to motivate your youngster. For instance, if they are hesitant to order ice cream, you could tell them that they must do it if they want it. Of course, you should only use this if you are confident in their ability to accomplish it independently.

1. Place a mattress on the floor next to your bed for your child to sleep on.
2. Allow your child to sleep on the floor, but put it closer to the middle and away from the bed.
3. Allow your child to sleep on a mat on the floor in the room, understanding that you will place them in their bed after they fall asleep.
4. Allow your child to fall asleep in their room with you present.
5. Allow your child to fall asleep in their room with the understanding that you will monitor them every few minutes until they fall asleep.
6. Allow your youngster to fall asleep with the light on in their room.
7. Allow your youngster to sleep with only a nightlight in their room.

Change the Channel

If your child is worrying about something they canot control, such as the possibility that it will rain tomorrow, causing a football match to be canceled, let them distract themselves.

"Is there something you can do about that?" ask your youngster when he or she is focused on a specific concern. If the answer is affirmative, assist them in resolving the issue.

For instance, studying might be an excellent idea if they are afraid of a science test. They could also practice their talents if they are afraid of not making the basketball squad.

If they are concerned about things they cannot control, such as the weather or another person's actions, remind them that the only thing they can handle is how they react. Discuss how they might deal with poor weather or how they could react if someone is cruel to them.

Then, assist them in diverting their attention away from the subject. Help them change channels to change the mood. Constant worrying will leave them caught in a state of tension.

Be Aware of Your Parenting Style

Because some parenting styles can exacerbate your child's anxiety, it's critical to examine your parenting style and relationships with your child. Both authoritarian and liberal parenting styles, according to psychologist Diana Baumrind, are associated with an increased incidence of depression and anxiety in children. Expecting perfection and having complete control over your child's actions is a definite way to cause worry in both yourself and your child. It can make your child feel pressurized to succeed all the time, leaving them immobilized with anxiety and self-doubt.

Boundary-free parenting, on the other hand, is rarely the solution. Permissive parenting devolves so much power to the child's decisions that it might cause uneasiness. Allowing their child to deal with life's everyday problems helps them build more resiliency and appropriate coping mechanisms.

AUTHORITATIVE
AUTHORITARIAN
PERMISSIVE
UNINVOLVED

The Take-Home Message

Consult a specialist if your child's anxiousness lasts longer than two weeks. If your child's anxiety is hurting with daily functioning, you should consult a psychiatrist.

For example, if their anxiety affects their school attendance or grades, or if they cannot participate in social activities due to their concerns, they may require professional assistance.

Anxiety disorders in children are prevalent. These include generalized anxiety disorder, post-traumatic stress disorder, chronic anxiety, and particular phobia. Around 4 million children aged three to seventeen years in the United States (almost 7 percent of the population) suffer from anxiety.

Anxiety disorders are relatively treatable, but they go undetected and unrecognized far too often. Consult your doctor if you suspect your child has an anxiety issue. Your child's physician may send him or her to a mental health specialist for help.

Each anxiety disorder has its list of symptoms and, as a result, treatment. Anxiety is usually treated with cognitive therapy, but it can also be treated with medication. A mental health expert can assist your child in developing skills to cope with anxious feelings and gaining confidence in confronting some of his anxieties.

A therapist will almost certainly want you to participate in treatment so that you may learn how to help your kid at home. You may learn particular ways to coach your child when they are worried, or you could learn how to help them healthily face their anxieties.

While dealing with your child's anxiety can be difficult and exhausting for many parents, the best part is that they can conquer it with this anxiety workbook. Following these strategies and providing connection and support to your child can go a long way toward empowering them. They will learn that their parents will listen to their problems and provide them with validation, tools, and assistance. Help your kids with the activities, exercises, and worksheets to deal with their anxieties.

Ingram Content Group UK Ltd.
Milton Keynes UK
UKHW021310130623
423377UK00023B/779

9 781956 223750